My copy

Lateral Thinking

Brandino Ragioni
Machiavelli

brandino.machiavelli@gmail.com
Tel. 07788691815

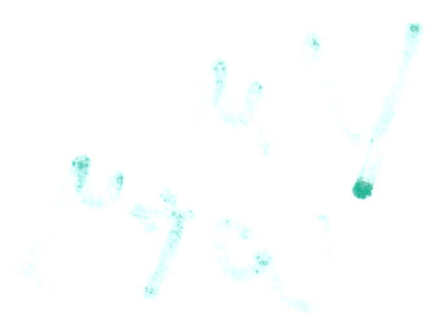

21st Century Madness

In a world where the opportunities to rejoice are reserved for feelings which are generally outside our day-to-day achievements, it cannot be surprising that two perfectly sane and civilised people like the two athletes pictured above are debased by an almost animal-like frenzy of anger at having finally achieved their objective. Human competition is carried to extremes, forced through by incredible pressures from the media, the public and the need for fame, and therefore hailed as Man's and Woman's greatest goal.

In today's world everything seems an impossible confusion. Every day I feel the confirmation that we are taking part in the birth of something great. I believe the tension of living has never been greater.
(Teilhard de Chardin, letter to Lucile Swan, 1936)

Verily God does not change the condition of a people until they change what is in themselves,
(Qur'an - 13:11).

LATERAL THINKING

Silenced Ethics in our Agnostic Era

A pamphlet

Brandino Rangoni Machiavelli

Edited by
Alberto Cuomo

Published in London, 2021

© 2021, Aldobrandino Rangoni Machiavelli

ISBN: 9798741578643

Contents

Preface 10

Introduction 12

1. The West is Best? 16
2. Our Civilisation, wonderful phenomenon full of faults. 32
3. Postscript 45

Appendix, Further Reading, Notes & Bibliography 53

Preface

This booklet is intended as a "Pamphlet" in the sense of being a brief introduction to the need for our Western culture, with its encompassing position in today's world, to become aware and to understand the need, and consequently to encourage the adoption of a new set of ethics based on a universal "faith" in the requirements for today's communitarian living. We can no longer ignore the numerous imbalances, myopia, corruption, abuse and general malpractice endorsed by custom and by law, all of which have now reached global dimension thanks to the success of globalisation. The human race is made up of inherently honest, but also highly constructive and innovative individuals who are prone to take full advantage of promising situations and opportunities. These have become, for better or for worse, vastly more available world-wide during the last decades, and urgently need new universal principles to keep them within the requirements of communal living. We have for too long assumed our Western culture to be the only viable one but have now reached a number of issues which will impact our social life, our security and even our existence if we procrastinate. We must now open our minds to new and fundamental directions for change. With intelligence. Without prejudice. And with humility.

Introduction
"Everything changes and nothing remains still" - Heraclitus.

Upheaval

At the beginning of ISIS' explosive drive into Iraq, a Pakistani immigrant friend living and working in Italy with his family for over a decade predicted that within 10 to 15 years, at the most, the conflict and strife that are rampant in Pakistan, Afghanistan, and the Middle East will have spread inevitably to the tranquil, prosperous hills of the Marche, in central Italy, where we were at the time all peacefully enjoying a sunny summer's afternoon drinking tea. What was perhaps most striking was that for him this version of the future was perfectly acceptable, or rather entirely possible based on his own experiences.

What to my perception was an imperfect but solid piece of the world's geography, my beautiful Italy, where one lives quite decently, within the rule of law and with valid hopes of maintaining one's lifestyle in our cosy European environment, to him was only another vulnerable part of a dangerous and frail world.

But we barely need to scratch the surface of the principles on which our society operates to discover serious and grave faults far greater than the threat of ISIS. In fact, my friend's fears are probably more founded than our certainties on the stability of our way of life. We are vulnerable on many fronts, politically, economically, and morally. Politics are run by individuals of little depth and foresight; our economies are frequently and increasingly functioning on a knife-edge; we are rapidly destroying our environment; we are depleting our resources; we are allowing our lives to be run by commercial greed; our educational system has dragged our social and intellectual manifestations to a frightening low level; we are allowing 21st century slavery to exist in our backyards. Our society has surely lost its way in the depths of its roots, its weaknesses sustained and hidden by an external gloss of success and an undeniably attractive display of wealth.

We are living in an increasingly fragile environment.

Can we, in the West, really be so sure that the unrest and pressure of millions of people living around us, added to the obvious, spreading dysfunctions of our own system of rapacious neo-liberal capitalism, will allow us to continue to wistfully mow our lawns, go on holidays, enjoy the security of our leafy middle-class existence indefinitely? Are we not resting on the unstable laurels of an incredibly rapid and successful spread of technological, economic, social advance, based on a massive disparity of opportunities, of wealth, of safety and well-being, due to the cynical exploitation of sections of our own society, and of those in other parts of the world?

But, as history and experience will teach us, dangers and disruptions are also chances for new opportunities. Change is inherent in every aspect of life, in every aspect of our universe. "Everything changes and nothing remains still" as the Greek Heraclitus said already 2500 years ago. It is up to us to transform a negative into a positive, and we must assume that a positive side is potentially always present in all that happens, if we have the insight and the courage to identify it. We are bound, not only in the West, but at some level in all societies and environments, to search for what can be developed into good from what appears to be an insoluble and extreme situation. The West has made gigantic strides towards technological development in all fields of science; it has allowed people to achieve a level of practical well-being never dreamt of before. But it is suffering from a diminishing sense of behavioural requirements which have created confusion, stress, and a widely spread lack of security both at social and at personal levels. We are still reeling from the end of the age-old support and certainty of religious belief which, for better and for worse, had sustained our actions and justified our existence to ourselves since the dawn of our humanity. The time has come for us to explore, accept, and somehow incorporate some of the principles which have allowed other civilisations to survive without the moral emptiness and the rat-race rush to illusory riches of all kinds which are characterising our culture. The alternative might, possibly, be to be wiped off the face of the Earth or to become overrun by wild murderous revolutionaries, which by then might not be hordes of jihadists but exasperated dwellers of our own urban culture. It is time to act.

This is not a scientifically researched book nor an attempt to outline a solution to our world-wide problems. My aim, spurred by the current intellectually stimulating discussions, projects, hopes and new awareness created by the Covid-19 global pandemic, is to give a brief and simple illustration of what I believe the problematic directions taken by our society are and attempt to highlight the unchanging truths that regulate our existence, which can inspire a new direction.

1. The West is Best?

The world is populated by over seven billion unique minds, countless languages, countless gods, habits, traditions. Scientists tell us that ethnic groups have been determined over the millennia by the environment, as humans have dispersed over the regions of the planet and adapted to what they found, or to the way the environment changed.

Over the centuries, Europeans and Northern Europeans in particular, have shown a propensity for developing a more materialistic, practical, comparatively less spiritual approach to culture than most other civilisations. They have rarely, if ever, come together as *Europeans*, and have, from early on, placed a high esteem on individuality. And this has allowed and encouraged, all across Europe, a high degree of individual creativity in the arts, the splendour and volume of which, I believe, has not been matched by any other culture, and rapidly accelerating technical achievements, which have possibly also encouraged confidence, aggressiveness and a seduction to conquest, discovery and eager curiosity. These, together with the capacity to imagine and develop an ever increasing and deadly array of arms and industries, resulted in the acquisition of power abroad and of high living standards at home convincing them that their way of life was the only one worth pursuing.

We in the West have for almost two hundred years, enjoyed unprecedented progress in terms of material well-being, which two horrendous and devastating world wars could not undo. Now we are being chastised for exceeding our self-indulgence and our presumption. After over two centuries of material pre-eminence and the development of highly sophisticated philosophical and psychological reasoning based on and validating their achievements, European cultures have come to something of a dead end. Or perhaps they reached a point where, like all things in this world, civilisations in particular, they have become worn out, and are in need of revitalisation in order to survive.

While science and technology have made enormous bounds of progress and success, the ethical standards of individuals have become secondary to monetary, personalised, egoistical pursuits. What used to be banded about as the primal principles that determined behaviour, at least in principle, has virtually disappeared from discourse.

In our time, corporations have effectively taken over the ruling of many secondary or less able countries, and powerful nations and their leaders are subject to the pressure of lobbying across different sectors from always greater dividend-seeking groups, ignoring, opposing and damaging to the public interest. Capitalism is close to becoming, has largely become, a dirty word.

The concept of democracy itself, admittedly only a couple of centuries old after the first ancient Athenian experience, seems to have lost its magical power to resolve all doubts on how to run a country.

All this has been recognised and written about by many sociologists, economists, and other pundits for a long time. "Secular liberalism", the Russian thinker Alexander

Herzen cautioned as early as 1862, "is the final religion, though its church is not of the other world but of this". Very few ideas have surfaced since the realisation by many thinkers that our Western system cannot keep growing forever, apart from being increasingly harmful in so many ways to society and to our planet. Nothing appears to be able to match the lure of material progress, made possible and irresistibly promoted by the increasing strength and monopolising power of global corporations, concentrating the world's wealth into the hands of a tiny number of huge entities which have the capacity to dictate our lives.

The more we become embroiled in this economy-led, consumer financed way of life called neo-liberalism the less we shall be able to take our own decisions and lead a life which can be based on democracy beyond economics.

"Democracy is the worst form of government, except for all the others." Winston S Churchill

"Democracy is a means, not an end."

"The liberty of a democracy is not safe if the people tolerated the growth of private power to a point where it becomes stronger than the democratic state itself. That in its essence is fascism: ownership of government by an individual, by a group, or any controlling private power."
— Franklin D. Roosevelt

A few words here from Wendy Brown, a "cutting edge" Political Theorist, make the point quite clearly:

"What happens when the precepts and principles of democracy are remade by [neo-liberalism]? When the

commitment to individual and collective self-rule and the institutions supporting it are overwhelmed and then displaced by the encomium to enhance capital value, competitive positioning, and credit ratings? What happens when the practices and principles of speech, deliberation, law, popular sovereignty, participation, education, public goods, and shared power entailed in rule by the people are submitted to economization?"
Excerpt from Undoing the Demos - Wendy Brown. Wendy Brown teaches political theory at the University of California, Berkeley

It certainly appears to me that a new direction is needed for societies both in the East and in the West to somehow reach a common approach to the development of a system that may – with all the difficulties, delays and mistakes inevitable in our human condition – achieve an improvement on human interaction in the wake of the unavoidable transformation of all our lives. The inexorable advance of globalisation, which has become one of the major threats to the survival of the qualities of lives manifested by countless different cultures could become a precious tool to unite our world into a common path towards this goal.

> **Democracy**
>
> Democracy is undoubtedly the most levelling solution to governing through the will of the people. But it has many limitations, particularly when numbers of the governed become large. Tantalisingly, the etymology of *'demos'* of *'democracy'* is Greek for 'district', a very recognisable description of a limited territory. We are today blinkered by our belief that we must be governed by democratically elected governments through a direct vote from all members of society, in whatever country and in spite of whatever social, historical and demographic situation this country is in. Without any pretence in offering a solution, I would like to dare here to 'out' this thought: that the principle of democracy needs to be preceded by higher, principled basic criteria. What really matters is that one group does not overcome another, that violence is not allowed to inhibit people's lives and freedom of action, speech and life choices. What matters is the attitude of people towards each other. What matters is that people feel and accept that others must be allowed space. What matters, in the end, is a sense of duty, towards individuals and towards society, that must be expected from governments as well as individuals. And an inherent and strong sense of duty can encompass any size of population, in fact should and must include all. Without all this, the democratic principle is just another way for ambitious politicians to coerce the 'masses', the ordinary citizen, to play by some rules even if one does not agree to them, because they have been voted by a largely 'unlearned' majority.

A massive task, no doubt. But one that, given that the slow but steadily diminishing influence of established and traditional religious faith in every-day life, can, to my mind, be resolved only by the acquisition of a new "faith" that can be increasingly shared, with time, by a large and influential part of humanity.

The seeds for such a new development have repeatedly been sown by many thinkers since ancient times; the Buddha preached that the way to liberation from human suffering is not through worship of a god or anything else but by becoming a fully autonomous and compassionate human being. The implication of the Buddha's logic is that even belief in God is a form of human desire and clinging, a product of the ego and another cause of suffering since it prevents a person from becoming an autonomous and free human being. Modern Japanese society for centuries has been largely free from the subjection to a God, although they have a pervasive spiritual sense of existence.

In the European tradition, and already within the epoch of our 'modern' culture, people of very different cultural provenance such as Kant the philosopher, Edward Gibbon the historian, Giuseppe Mazzini the politician, Teilhard de Chardin the theologian, and many others, last but not least Stephen Hawkin the scientist, have expressed the principle of a connection, a commonality and a possible explanation of our existence situated somewhere between materialistic reasoning and a supernatural 'will', an undefinable, universal 'energy' which we have so far called God, which is an etymological derivation of a Sanskrit root *gheu(e)*- "to call, invoke" – a very human, very predictable call for help from a race of beings who have understood and have become conscious of their frailty.

It is undeniable that human "progress" has gone too far in its material development while remaining behind at the moral level. We have developed a capacity for uncontrollable greed and have totally failed to identify its limiting and self-destructive nature.

In my opinion, the major underlying cause of all these issues is the lack of a generalised sense of what are the requirements, the basic rules, the boundaries of communal living. The modern age has almost forgotten that there are ethical principles that need to be respected for society to be able to function in a coherent way. Not that they have ever reached a position of dominance in human society. But religious faith has, until recently, been a powerful deterrent to the majority of those intent to ignore the principles of coexistence and of communitarian rules. Religious faith has been identified with custom. It has never been a great obstacle to those in power either; but there was always the possibility, the fear, of being punished. And more importantly, the means of coercion, disguise, dissimulation and dependency of society achieved by powerful, often global, entities have never been as strong as they are today.

I believe we must set ourselves the task of helping our society, starting from ourselves, to change our perspective on life through example and education by highlighting the faults of our currently overpowering, freewheeling, confused cultural environment, as well as give an outline to potential ways forward.

Extract from An Essay on the Duties of Man - *Giuseppe Mazzini (1856)*

I believe this 150 year-old quote from Giuseppe Mazzini, a pre-eminent Italian 19th century thinker, freedom fighter, and politician, is worth including here, as an example and a testimonial of the long-standing sentiments of a man of vision: it is a heartfelt appeal with admirable foresight about duty as a principle of life, addressed to the nascent new States of the time which, while aiming to finally adopt after centuries of oppression the principles of the French Revolution, were in danger of becoming overwhelmed by the advance of the dark unprincipled forces of commercial exploitation and political embezzlement through the cracks of democracy.

[....] All that has been achieved or attempted in the cause of progress and improvement in Europe during the last fifty years, [....], has been attempted in the name of the Rights of Man and of Liberty, as the means of that well-being which has been regarded as the end and aim of life. All the acts of the great French Revolution, and of all those revolutions which succeeded and imitated it, were a consequence of the "Declaration of the Rights of Man." All the works of those philosophers, whose writings prepared the way for that Revolution, were founded upon a theory of Liberty, and of making known to every individual his Rights. The doctrines of all the Revolutionary schools preached that man was born for happiness; that he had a right to seek happiness by every means in his power; and that no one had a right to impede him in that search; while he had a right to overthrow whatever obstacles he met in his path towards it.
[.....] Has the condition of the people improved? Have the millions who live by the daily labour of their hands acquired any, the smallest amount, of the promised and desired well-being?
No; the condition of the people is not improved. [.....] In almost all countries the condition of the workingman has become more uncertain, more precarious, while those crises which condemn thousands of workingmen to a certain period of inertia have become more frequent.

And nevertheless, in these last fifty years the sources of social wealth and the mass of material means of happiness have been continually on the increase. [....]

(Giuseppe Mazzini, An Essay On the Duties of Man Addressed to Workingmen in New York in 1858. Published by Funk & Wagnalls, 1898) [i]

Rights and Duties

In nature, there are no rights. There are only the results of slow, determined, intelligent, ceaseless moves and choices which procure a temporary place in the universe. The survival of the fittest, as this is called, is not the survival of the most ferocious or the most violent, it is the survival of the one who has put in place the better solution to its survival. For the tiger, it is a combination of sophisticated hunting techniques and physical strength. For the antelope, it is speed and the 'safety in numbers' principle, a technique anything but aggressive. For plants, it can be pervasiveness, the capacity to diffuse seed widely. For humans, it is the community. If a man goes hungry, he has no inherent, absolute right to expect to be fed. It is the duty of others, of his family, of his neighbours, of whoever comes in contact with him, including his government, to feed him. No one has an inherent right to a fair trial. It is the moral duty of the community to provide a legal system that will provide him with one.

You can thrive as a humble employee, or as a soldier, or as a merchant or scientist or farmer and so on. You can survive in spite of being poor if you are resourceful or if you live in a society which helps the less fortunate. You can become rich if you have the right social position and you are determined, strong and aggressive. There are no inherent rights involved in these outcomes. The individual in South East Asia who has nothing to eat has no inherent right to be fed, in the same way that the individual living in the least privileged areas of the vastly populated metropolis in Sub-Saharan Africa, or the beggar on our street, doesn't. Just as no other element in nature has any inherent right to exist but keeps doing its best to keep alive and prosper. Humans have, from the very beginning, thrived on communal life. This has resulted in the principle of duty: in order to survive in our environment, we must look after our kin and the environment itself. And since this may not always be in our personal interest it must become a recognised duty.

Eclipse of spirituality

Spirituality[ii] is the human attribute which gives us the gift of peace. It has nothing to do with worrying if we will go to heaven or hell. It has nothing to do directly with making efforts to better ourselves; bettering ourselves is a consequence of spirituality.

Western/American culture, now encompassing most of the planet's regions and certainly all of those aiming to improve the livelihood of its inhabitants, for no alternative and viable means of increasing the material welfare of populations has so far been found, has gone through rapid periods of change since its beginning at the start of the 19th century. Spirituality has not been immune, and although I am in no position to make an informed analysis of these developments, I believe it is possible to identify certain of its basic characteristics in the last hundred years or so.

At the beginning of the 20th century spirituality in Europe and in the West in general was considered to be pervasive of society. After all, it had been ostensibly the source of all thinking for at least one thousand years, and much longer. It was religious-based and was expected to be recognised and practiced by all. In Asia it could be said that it was even frequently the ruler of society translated through the various forms of religious beliefs and representatives of power.

With the ascent of material wealth in Europe, peoples' dependency on spirituality in matters of every-day life decreased in favour of the results which could be obtained from new forms of recently introduced entities such as representative governments, industry and commerce. In the rest of the world little changed except for the considerable influence of colonial powers which brought the evolution of their way of thinking with them.

In the latter four or five decades or so, spirituality in Western cultures has been not negated but forced underground by what is known with the vague denomination of "the Economy". The principle of a State driven by an efficient economic system has no space for spiritual obstacles to the development of fast growing, money-making, opportunity seeking activities. It must simply obey the laws of business, and neglect and impede whatever stands in its righteous way to satisfying the needs of the population. This is particularly true in societies such as the American which is founded on immigration.

Emigration and Regions

Emigration has characterised the last two centuries and is constantly increasing in volume and in geographical extension. Poverty following the increases in population, and the relative poverty perceived by people living in primitive surrounding, dazzled by tales of riches elsewhere has given hope to millions. The diffusion of TV and mobile phones has given people the mirage of a better life elsewhere. The wrenching away from their original culture and geographical environment has badly dented the self-reliance of millions of people, who have been forced to adopt different ways of living and behaving, often, if not always, very different from the principles of ethics learned at home: principles which were considered immovable and almost sacred. In such a situation the loosening and loss of focus on ethics is practically obligatory. One of the most interesting characteristics of geographical regions is their rough similarity in size. Regions can be small or large, but they do not seem to vary in size beyond a certain limit. The size of Yorkshire is not all that different from that of Tuscany. This characteristic is the result of the physical limits of human interaction among communities, which is true both in terms of distance and in terms of numbers of individuals. Plato, in his book Republic, stated an exact number (5040) as the ideal figure for a community in order to be controllable and self-sufficient. Regions are the basis of our culture. Humanity has developed on a regional basis; all cultures, all points of reference by which we recognise ourselves as 'belonging' are based on family and on extended families, which are ultimately the region in which we have developed, where our family developed, where we have our 'roots'. We cannot transcend from this. And yet, regions have been virtually neglected until recently as entities of any importance, in the rush towards development and higher standards of living, by those who determine our lifestyles and ostensibly 'lead'.

The scale of reference of historians goes from families to the State, leaving the regional dimension out. Politicians are bound to make Regions are the most typical and significant geographical area where local characteristics tend to evolve. Over generations, attitudes, beliefs, language, and much more are embedded into the daily life of children, who in turn pass on these useful, comforting and security-enhancing bits of knowledge. The way your mother kissed you good night can be a source of great relief to a lonely person far from home.

A region can be described as a geographical area which is characterised by how its inhabitants live within it, as well as by its geographical characteristics, which has contributed to determining their lifestyle. To be defined as an area, a region must have boundaries of some description. These boundaries, however, although they are often defined by a large plain, a range of mountains, a stretch of coast, a forest or a desert, are not always self-evident geographically, and can then be defined in human terms by the different language, living habits, culture, economic activities, or political organisation of the inhabitants of one region in relation to the regions next to it. Thus a region is not only a geographical term, but also a cultural one, although the two generally go together, since the creation of a culture within a region is due to the fact that its community has developed in some degree of isolation from its surrounding humanity.

reference to their whole State, which they have been elected to represent in its entirety.

The statement that our planet is a living organism is appealing, but misleading. It gives the impression that as a consequence the concept of the 'global village' is one that responds to a natural dimension and should be encouraged as the answer to our problems of development, inequalities, pollution and localised poverty and richness. Our planet should be described as a collection of or a family of living organisms, where each has its own environment, ambitions and reasons for living.

For the past 500 years, in the Western world, mankind has been widening the confines of its regional coverage. The time has (long) come when this coverage has become far too large to encompass. At

> first, small nation-states acquired more and more territories for purpose of conquest and power and in order to safeguard their frontiers. These enlarged regions became known as Nation-states, and in the last 200 years, Nation-states have been hyped up as the 'fatherland' by politicians and by people in power who had a vested interest in promoting the idea that the State was the most important thing in a man's life. Even worth dying for. But in reality, the concept of a nation state has mostly remained superficial. An Englishman or a Frenchman will display a strong sense of nationalism in a crisis (be it a war or a football tournament) but their habits and temperament will still be traceable to a particular region. And nine times out of ten, the individual will be proud of them.
>
> Regions have become more blurred over the years in certain areas. This has been largely based on historical facts that have determined an increasing homogeneity among the people inhabiting an area. England, for instance, has many of the characteristics of a 'region' even though it is as large as an average 'country'. And in fact, its people have had a homogeneous government for longer than almost any other state in Europe. Tuscany, on the other hand, is a region of more average dimensions. The reason for this is its geography and its social history, bound to the temperament of its inhabitants and to the succession of invasions and political changes that have characterised its existence. Even 900 years of stable government have not cancelled the distinguishing characteristics which place a Yorkshireman and a man from Devon apart. Larger social and geographical entities, the 'nation-states' which are the norm today, are only justified in terms of political and military clout, which is greater than that of regions for sheer questions of size.

There is an uncompromising opposition of principles between spirituality and the way our modern society operates. This opposition has always been present between the principles of living outlined by religion and the realities of life, but until the overpowering influence of modern industrial commerce, it had always been at least formally recognised. Today, the principles of following a path of continual enrichment and illusory happiness imply that they also enclose the aspirations of spirituality. In reality, this State-induced spirituality is as shallow and 'canned' a product as a can of beans.

Again, I would like to quote Wendy Brown here, since being a political theorist writing on the perils of neo-liberalism she may be considered outside of any religious debate. "*[....] Economic criteria [today] are supposed to be enough to drive society and give a better life to all, from all aspects: social, educational, medical, ; spirituality in this context virtually disappears, since there is no space for it in the life of such a society, and theoretically no need.*

Countering this tendency, which dehumanises society and eclipses the individual as a thinking being, may take decades or centuries. It is bound to happen, even once the system has taken hold completely, unless the process is so thorough and unforgiving that a new breed of humans emerges with a totally different set of principles and aims in life.

But in this, our beginning of century this phenomenon is still in a relatively undeveloped stage. It is possible to extract ourselves from it through presenting a new outlook on life which is however based on our existing traditions and principles. These principles are very simply the principles which, in theory, govern our life today. They are the principles of freedom and happiness. The principles of living according to what all societies have tried to achieve, justice, peace, and personal development."
(Undoing the Demos – Wendy Brown)

The eclipse in spirituality is one of the reasons why ethics have been able to be pushed aside. Our lives, filled with material preoccupations have no room left to practice the art of leaving our cares aside and thinking in a detached way about what is beyond us, near us, and who and what we ourselves are. If we were able to do so we would understand the need for ethics to steer us through our lives, and we would have the time to acquire the understanding of what ethics are. We urgently need to sit back, and wonder.

What are the ethics of today in our Christian society? Are they still following the ten commandments of Christian tradition, the tradition which in theory informs our Western civilisation? And are they still valid?

Here they are:

1. *Thou shalt have no other Gods before Me*
    Has anyone except a priest ever openly stated this principle to us?

2. *Thou shalt not make unto thee any graven image*
    When was the last time this commandment of God was ever discussed, let alone followed?

3. *Thou shalt not take the name of the Lord thy God in vain*
    Swearing is socially frowned upon, but not taken seriously by most.

4. *Remember the sabbath day and keep it holy*
    If it means going to church, they are emptying.

5. *Honour thy father and thy mother*
    We would love to but unfortunately, we don't have the time.

6. *Thou shalt not kill*
    Nothing has changed in the last 2000 years. If anything, things have gotten worse.

7. *Thou shalt not commit adultery*
    Times have changed! People are free to decide.

8. *Thou shalt not steal*
    We just unjustifiably acquire other people's money in more sophisticated ways in order to get richer.

9. *Thou shalt not bear false witness against thy neighbour*
    It is mostly Justice that restrains us, not our principles.

10. *Thou shalt not covet anything that is thy neighbour's*
    We just get a better one.

And what about Christ himself and all he said about love, forgiveness, and the camel and needle thread? I would never wish to judge people for their lack of adherence to these dictates and teachings. But how can we still declare that we are Christians? Or should the Commandments of Moses just be declared obsolete? It is a subject way beyond my capabilities to tackle.

Ethics have changed over time, reflecting the customs of the ages. Today, we in the West have a set of ethics, based on the Christian ones, but they have become unwritten rules which are considered as given, principles which we acquire from education, experience, and our family environment. Their "disobedience" is not in any way considered as ruled by any law, much less imposed by religion, but are adhered to because they form a part of our knowledge about how to behave in life. This gives them a very great amount of leeway. We feel allowed to stretch their significance and somehow evade the necessity of their application, on the basis of other issues, customs or needs.

I am not a preacher. My aim is to suggest that we have some serious and well-recognised problems: overpopulation, wars, violence, climate change, the destruction of our planet's finite resources, a general uncertainty and confusion. All such problems deliver us into the hands of a few unscrupulous, arrogant and power-hungry entities and individuals who are deaf and blind to the world beyond their restricted "bubble" of interest. It is becoming urgent to take some strong initiatives to begin to resolve these problems, which have all, in my opinion, a common origin: the lack of strong but simple basic ethical principles which can govern our behaviour.

2. Our Civilisation, a most wonderful phenomenon full of faults

Western civilisation has for the last couple of hundred years gradually reduced to lip service or dismissed the rules which through Nature keep a frail but constant balance in our world. We are defying them at our peril, as many signs are now showing us, exchanging them with our own man-made rules borne of our own successful material and intellectual achievements. We have been disregarding the requirements for our common survival on, and in harmony with, our planet. We have ignored or forgotten, throughout history and with the conviction that our Gods had manufactured the Universe for our exclusive consumption, the limits of our environment. We have lost all measures of greed, violence, pain, extermination, in relation to our fellowmen and to our planet as a whole.

As mentioned, this has been lamented by many writers, scholars and thinkers. But no one has yet outlined any sort of new direction that can get us out of an impasse which is soon to be reached by continuing to follow the dead ends that we are reaching. That is because no one has tried to ask the basic question. Nobody has tried to tackle the source of the problem; the question has always been "what to do", and never "why is it happening".

One of the ways to try to understand this is to look at what other human communities are doing. For we must not forget that our way of life is not unique. In spite of its overwhelming inroad into virtually all societies, there are still many different ways in which people successfully think and organise their lives. In the West, making money may be the prime choice; it may also be playing football or having a nice house or travelling. But in parts of Asia it might be praying in a temple, or preparing for a daughter's wedding. I think it can be said, within a large approximation, that for most people outside of Western culture making money is probably a very real concern but not the primary choice or desire.

In spite of the strong growth of economies which have adopted to a greater or lesser degree an American lifestyle and experienced its initial benefits, the limits of capitalism are becoming more apparent in those areas where it has developed most. The capitalist system, based on the principle of allowing the 'markets' to regulate themselves, dictates that freedom must be allowed to be able to develop in order to increase the wealth of society as a whole: initially, capitalism has done this very well, which is why it is so popular and its sister principle, the government by democracy, is such a winning proposition throughout the world at present.

But capitalism has two serious flaws: it does not distribute its riches equally; and it assumes a dedication to making money which is directly related to the amount of success you obtain in life. Both these factors imply that if one person is successful another must necessarily be less so. For it is being increasingly proven that it is not possible to advance in a capitalist society without stepping on someone else's toes (as an example, see "What is the Ideal Unemployment Rate" article in Appendix). It's a fact of life. It has always been so since human societies have begun, and more so since they began to be so populous that room for expansion beyond their territories proved increasingly difficult if not impossible. Capitalism is the human, legalised embodiment of the principle in nature of the survival of the fittest, where "the fittest" is no longer the one who can best provide for his own personal needs (and those of his immediate companions), but the one who has accumulated the most value in a system which has developed a surplus of goods. In this environment, all religion, which by definition preaches brotherhood, goodness, restraint, honesty, respect, is put at a disadvantage, since to function properly capitalism requires egotism, disregard for feelings, working to the limits of legality, greed, and disregard for others' needs. Meritocracy is a typical syndrome of these unwritten axioms.

Meritocracy

Meritocracy, considered one of the pillars of modern successful societies, has proven to be a tool for the exclusion of the most for the advantage of the few. Individuals who deserve to advance in society are by a very large proportion derived from the wealthy classes, who have access to better education, more contacts, greater financial means. The rest, the vast majority, are left aside. Not only: they are also considered by society as inherent failures, those who did not make it, those who did not have the capacity or the will to "succeed". Meritocracy has introduced a principle of individualism brought to its extremes. If you can beat the system, you are praised: legality becomes not a tool for protection but something to overcome. Meritocracy often does not reward honesty but gain. It has always been so, of course, but until our God ruled our consciences restraint was imposed or practiced by all except the true buccaneers of society[1]. It is a powerful engine for

---

[1] Buccaneers, from Julius Caesar the conqueror to Henry Ford the automobile mogul have always been the movers of societies. But their greatness has inherently included a greater sense of their

> industrial development, but it has created a social community where personal skill is nurtured and used in promoting and realising potentially lucrative activities and managing the people who can realise them. This community is focused on such activities' potential return in prestige and money and has no compunction in exploiting whatever is necessary to achieve its aims. Business in the developed and developing world has changed the way people talk, act and even words have acquired a different meaning. It is interesting to see how the definition of power has shifted over the last 60 years in this one example among many:
>
> | Synonyms for the word POWER in 1955 in Webster's Dictionary | Synonyms for the word POWER in 2020 Thesaurus.com |
> |---|---|
> | Authority | Capability |
> | Jurisdiction | Capacity |
> | Control | Function |
> | Command | Influence |
> | Dominion | Potential |
>
> In 1955 the emphasis was on tangible, practical examples of power, mostly understood to be finalised and in the hands of the bureaucracy; the relationship with the rest of the community was built-in and essential. In 2020 the concept of power is exclusively on potential, personally developed abilities which do not necessarily have a connection with the rest of society. Nor do they have any connection at all with ethics, unless they become useful for some specific, usually transitory, requirement.

Since its establishment in the late Imperial Rome as an influential and politicised State Church, Christianity has accompanied, encouraged and sustained all forms of secular power games including wars, colonialism, and exploitation. However, since the beginning of the 20th century, it has lost much of its moral force in most developed societies, brought down partly by its contradictions and its pervasive alliance with materialism,

---

human position in the world. Caesar, for the glory of the Roman Empire; Ford, to give Americans an accessible means of transport.

but mostly because it gets in the way of our modern daily existence. The West, lacking anything capable of applying its own Christian moral principles, has become like a massive and unwieldy piece of ethical debris, without direction. It does not fall into chaos simply, in my belief, because the vast majority of humanity has innate principles of fairness and honesty and compassion which sustain it. Humans instinctively know what is right. Society then forces them to abandon their instincts and follow the rules which allow the "system" as a whole to function. Individualism breaks communities and forces people to compete against one another while enslaving themselves to massive organisations which have the power to suspend their livelihood at an hour's notice.

As the author George Monbiot says in his book "How did we get into this mess?"[iii]

This is the Age of Loneliness. [...] In the past few years we have seen loneliness become an epidemic among young adults. Now we learn that it is just as great an affliction for older people. [...] The war of every man against every man – competition and individualism, in other words – is the religion of our time, justified by a mythology of lone rangers, sole traders, self-starters, self-made men and women, going it alone. For the most social of creatures, who cannot prosper without love, there is now no such thing as society, only heroic individualism. (George Monbiot – How Did We Get Into This Mess?)

What is however obvious is that some kind of 'faith' in something beyond and outside us has and continues to be necessary for humanity to get on with their lives. In pre-historic times it seems that natural objects, relevant to the people involved, were considered sacred. This did not concern or threaten the original equilibrium, an always evolving but perfected balance of the environment; nor ostensibly the relationship between humans. Gradually, as society became more complex, the manifestations of the Divine came to include increasingly complex aspects of behaviour. These became complicated and lost their direct relationship with practical circumstances. A solid precept, simple in its obvious original form, is difficult to follow if society allows you to act in a way where you have to make that decision yourself, and the consequences of your decision might be felt very far from your immediate interest. Ethics, the source of inspiration for countless daily decisions, can become intangible, even disappear altogether.

A New Chapter

Nature does not work with an end in view. For the eternal and infinite Being, which we call God or Nature, acts by the same necessity as that whereby it exists [...]. Therefore, as He does not exist for the sake of an end, so neither does He act for the sake of an end; of His existence and of His action there is neither origin nor end. [iv. Preface]. God is indifferent to individuals. God is without passions, neither is he affected by any emotion of pleasure or pain. Strictly speaking, God does not love anyone. [V.17]. He who loves God cannot endeavor that God should love him in return.

(Spinoza – Ethics, Part 4)

I think at this point I would like to clarify my definition of faith. For my previous statements would normally be misinterpreted as those of an atheist. There are countless "Faiths" on our planet, and they represent individual or community or cultural beliefs which are essential pillars for a balanced and just journey through life. The deeply established need for human beings to keep themselves afloat in the world while also pursuing love in the widest possible meaning of the term determines the need to be able to look to something universal which can justify their innumerable quests in life. Strong individuals may aim for personal power while a larger number will find an umbrella under which to find one's destiny and desires. But we all need something. And there is a very wide range to choose from, some wonderfully, in fact one is tempted to say divinely, elaborated, others more primitive. Current faiths are, in my opinion, intimately based on culture, which is based on genes, which is based on the development of groups of humans according to their geographical and historical background.

Faith is based on genes and background. And although this may not strike a chord with many, I am convinced that anyone's instinctive feelings, in the best days, are essentially exactly the same as everybody else's fundamental feelings of inner faith. And I cannot help but believing that any expression of faith, in whatever form, when examined is an expression of our belonging to a universal, unique entity far beyond the narrow confines of any provincial, regional, purpose-made religion.

My personal Faith is that there certainly is an Entity, or God, that rules our lives. This Entity is sometimes reachable by ourselves through what we call 'prayer', but not in the way that we think: our prayers may be fulfilled, but not because there is a God who listens to our invocation, but because of our capability to convince ourselves that our belief has fulfilled it. If there is power in prayer it is surely the strength of the belief that God is listening. My own belief is that our invocation is not personal but responds to something different, something which has not (ever yet) been established. So 'what difference does it make?' one might ask. No difference at all, save that we should abandon our conviction that God is 'our' God. He is not. The God who is called upon to help an army win a battle or save a vessel from sinking is the same God who is invoked by the opposing side, the same God who will create the wave that will sink the vessel drowning all on board. The efficacy and outcome of our prayers depends on ourselves. We just have no idea of how far our capacity goes.

There are universal laws which govern our existence and which we are constrained to live within. These laws are set out, in one way or the other, in all documents created by exceptional individuals, in all ages and places, who have tried to teach their fellow humans how to behave in order to lead a just and peaceful life. They address the local condition of humankind and state how to solve the problems which affect their own life and that of their society on a daily basis. These precepts always address the same issues which, in different forms, are present and persistent in all human societies: cruelty, greed, ambition, indifference, hate. Because of their universality, and in order to be able to hope to achieve them, it has always been necessary to refer to an entity which is beyond the reach of humans, be they *paupers* or *kings*. And the obvious entity to refer to has always been something called God, which since the beginning of human time has represented the power of all things unknowable, from lightning to the cruel fate of unlucky humans.

The concept of God, typically undefinable, as well as providing an invaluable foundation of reassuring hope and a source of much good, has unfortunately been the root of unending problems, in all ages and cultures. It has been consistently misused by people who have imagined and imposed an all-too-human answer to the toils of life. It has been misused by people in power to advance their cause. It has served to subject and humiliate enemies. It has been the cause for the majority of wars and conflict and slaughter during the length of our history.

I believe the time has come to begin the transformation of our perception of God as the source of our moral directions into a more realistic, universal and attainable source of knowledge as opposed to myth and often bigoted religious dogmas. It is wrong and misleading to think that without our Gods our lives become steeped into chaos, desperation and evil. The contrary is true. The fundamental principles of life are there to be adopted through an understanding of how the universe itself operates, and our position in it, without the intermediary of religious faith.

Our conceptualisation of the principles of generosity, love, forgiveness, justice, and restraint, which we appear to have developed over the course of our species' relatively brief existence, is only the manifestation of the complexities of our minds, rendered extremely sophisticated by civilisation. We have a single word which can sum up these principles: ethics. A word which has often been avoided and neglected as if we were ashamed of uttering such a value-laden concept, distant as it is from all the pressing choices we need to make in order to achieve our aims in life. The fear of God and his punishments has theoretically kept us (at times, barely) in our place until a couple of hundred years ago. I believe we now urgently need a new faith, based on the same principles of all religious beliefs, including fairness, justice, generosity, respect and, above all, love, but originating from outside the concept of an omnipotent figure which is supposed to rule our lives, and rather founded on the principle that there is, indeed, an overarching entity which governs all our existences to the minutest details, but one that operates within extremely precise rules of conduct which are inalterable. The figure of the Gods of yesterday and today, often represented in human form, and always represented with human principles, created to satisfy human needs, is the projection of our own needs, desires, fears, plans, insecurity and much else. The presence of different Gods, separate Deities representing a specific culture, Christian, Muslim, Hindi, or other, has dominated our lives, and no doubt greatly assisted us in many ways in the past. Today however, this image is less and less invoked by mankind, overcome by science and largely ignored by the busy world. And so it should be, although we should also be aware of the fact that there must be surely a universal power, be it divine or physical, which regulates every movement of the Universe. Science is looking for it, in the absence of contemporary thinkers, and if and when someone should find it, they can surely give it the worthy title of God. But it will be a Universal God, not a provincial fatherly autocrat in the model of an authoritarian paternalistic tribal chief.

Our human limitations have so far kept us from going beyond this narrow definition of God, which is the root of all the often unreasonable – and so many times wonderful – expectations, developments, actions, and inspirations, which have characterised our cultures everywhere. We have seldom imagined that the 'holiness' of our existence is not to be found in the generosity, anger, or whim of an Entity which acts on us as a Lord or a Father, but to our own, intellectual human development from the first life form to the contradictory, baffling but undoubtedly fascinating beings we are today. We underestimate ourselves. For it is we, human beings, who have had the extraordinary capability of understanding, imagining, interpreting, and developing the basic rules of communal living; it is we who have had the revelation that the rules which were being laboriously assembled over countless generations for or communal living were based on something beyond our control, immutable. Over time, since Nature then was not subject to our control, its definition was changed from "Nature" to "God": the figure of a personality which was closer to man and, possibly, with our increasing belief in the contradicting principles of the lofty imagination of poetry and the strength of arrogance, more approachable. But in this we grossly overestimate ourselves.

The master of our and everything else's fate, is, very simply and clearly, the laws by which the Universe is ruled. We have no idea of the origin of such laws, and some scientists even believe they may one day result in being the manifestation of a Creator. Whatever their origin, they are laws without which we and our Universe could not exist as we do and it does, and they have been the cause, and the origin of all the ethical principles we live by. Ethics are the human translation of the laws of Nature, of which the simplest and perhaps most inclusive and convincing definition is that of "Being", "To Be". When given a human connotation, Being is the contrary of Not Being, Destruction. Being cannot justify theft, murder, violence and destruction. But neither can it justify pain, exclusion, and fear. For the core of the principle of Being is not anger or hate, but Love, in the meaning of wanting to keep and create. It can, and has, become a set of universal rules as penned by our prophets, sages, buddhas of all denominations.

That law is everywhere, in every pebble and in every thought. In every cloud and in all the emptiness of the universe. It governs all because IT[iv] – capitalised here to give it some form of depiction, and to somehow distance it from our humanised Gods - is Nature, IT is Spirituality, IT is Time and Space and Past and Present and Future. IT is not good or evil. IT simply is. Every act that happens originates from IT, every wave of the ocean moves because of IT. Because IT is everything, the act, the wave, the force that drive both and everything else, IT will not intervene when a new born baby tragically dies because IT is the virus that killed it, IT is the car that hit it, IT is its death. How can we presume otherwise? What sense does it make to blame IT? And if we, who as IT *are* part of God ("close to Him (IT) as our jugular vein" – a famous saying in the Islamic Qur'an) as much as anything else in creation, take it upon ourselves to do something good, or bad, it is only ourselves that we can praise, or blame. But what we should not forget is that it is IT, in the form of our feelings, thoughts, emotions, that determines what we do. When some of us assume that we have a measure of freedom of action and of thought, we must remember that IT is freedom; whatever we decide is nothing more than an interpretation of IT; *our* will lies within ITs parameters. Which are the laws of the universe which we can call God.

If we take this reasoning to its logical conclusion, we immediately see how there can be no contradiction between science and religion. The two are, very simply, one. Science, the rational explanation; religion, the emotive, one. The main difference between the two is perhaps that it is 10,000 years or more that we have been mesmerised by our own multi-faceted constructions of the figure of a God who rules us in an entirely human fashion; while we have only just begun to scratch the surface of a scientific explanation of creation.

In reality, the apparently unsurmountable positioning between our humanised God and the universal IT/Entity is much closer than it seems. What we need to understand is that we have evaded the purpose of nature's path. We have given ourselves, in our profound ignorance, an importance within the universe which is entirely disproportionate. If we are able to accept the reality of the measure of our importance in the Universe. If we are able to accept our dependence from the laws which intimately govern us and everything else. If we can become aware, by directly experiencing them, the dangers to our environment but just as much our own, personal decline and enfeeblement of our moral values, both resulting from the same source. Only then will we be able to easily transfer the indubitable necessity and demand for belief, from the limited to the universal. Through this transference, which will include each and every of the requirements and wishes for a good and fair life as individuals and within the rest of the world, we shall be able to create an environment capable of managing our self-fulfilment and a globalised society. We must be ready to believe in a Universal God, which scientists can already tell us is the same for all mankind because it rules everything and everybody.

Lateral thinking

The way to begin entering a path to this end rests, in my opinion, on our capacity to simplify our principles and base them on few, solid ethical assumptions on how to rule our lives, strongly based on our "faith", belief, and understanding that we are following the laws of the one, universal, ruler of the Universe: the IT[v] or whatever name one gives it. These principles have been taught, preached, exhorted by many, and have been the basis for all sacred books. They inform the well-known Buddhist, Hindu, Shinto cultures, but also virtually every single body of humans who have developed a communal society. They have been spelled out centuries ago in the sacred books of our cultural background, the Torah, the New Testament and the Qur'an, all of which stem from a common fountainhead, the Bible. The fact that humanity has established these principles of communal living is proof of human ingenuity and genius; but it is above all a proof that they are universal necessities for survival. We, today, conscious of our advanced capabilities, but by no means immune from the universal principles of decay and extinction, must ask ourselves "why" our wrong directions have occurred in order to understand "how" they can be overcome. We shall soon establish that we are neglecting some rules of communal living which are also being ignored because of the scale and the complexity of our society, unable to correct itself. We must face the difficult task of admitting our weaknesses, reinforce our moral standing and enter a new chapter equal to the stage of development that we have reached.

3. Postscript

It is a mistake to think of the Islamic as one of the several ways of being religious. Rather, for fourteen centuries the Islamic has been one of the salient ways of being human. (Wilfred Cantwell Smith, "Islamic History as a Concept," in William Cantwell Smith, On
Understanding Islam: Selected Studies, The Hague: Mouton, 1981, 3–25, at 12.)

It is certainly not my presumption to have the capability of outlining a new way of life, or Heaven forbid a new religion. But I believe it is possible to lift some general basis of what the building blocks might be, from traditions and experience, which may give us guidance. Remaining within our monotheistic environment, my ignorance of the Torah does not allow me to cite it as a source of what a new faith might look like, or where to look for inspiration. Christianity, which undoubtedly includes all the right principles of a good life has, as outlined above, lost much of its credibility as a source of inspiration because of its political and moral degradation over the centuries. What is necessary first of all, in any case, is to come to an acceptance of a global Entity, an IT, which can be accepted by all; and Islam, created as it was, as a "completion" and a "final development" of the Jewish and Christian faiths derived from the Bible, is probably the one nearest to this approach. There is a lot that it can teach us.

Loyalty to 'God' over loyalty to the State

This is one of the slogans of the fearsome Islamic ISIS. But it is also an integral principle of Islam. And it has what I consider to be an expression of a fundamental truth: simply that good living, and healthy principles, are far more important than loyalty to a government or a system which can and is almost inevitably imperfect. It is useful to place this statement here because it can begin to exemplify the fact that Islam:
   a. is not a war-mongering organisation searching for world power (contrary to ISIS' belief),
   b. shows its capacity to criticise its own rulers,
   c. has a universal view of what the world might look like if it was governed by non-material principles.

It is in this context that the value of geographically defined entities as "regions" as opposed to "States" is useful. The statement is also a typical expression of Islamic suppleness and independence from earthly constraints. The fact that it has been hijacked by people like ISIS for a declaration of their military conquest of the world, to me is irrelevant. But its fundamental truth is unquestionable. Islamic thought rejects the principle of self-governing States and encourages the belief in a God who governs all peoples. I believe it cannot be denied that, bringing this statement to its lay meaning, it would certainly be advantageous if in a future globalised world, all communities had the same universal laws to respect.

One of the unique characteristics of the Islamic belief is in the details in which everyday behaviour in life is specified. This has probably come to the detriment of the Islamic culture itself because it tied it too closely with religious imperatives and consequently was often outpaced by the passing of time and habits, but it has also steadily shaped the lives of millions who to this day respect, by and large, its values and are guided by them within their ability and their strength all over the world with remarkable tenacity. We, in the West, can gain from observing how most of these shared precepts express their application with a sense of confidence and understanding, rather than as dogmas which threated eternal hell if disobeyed. Their secret lies in their simplicity.

Here are some examples. But the real examples come mostly from the way in which Muslims apply these teachings to everyday life.

"Be kind, honourable and humble to one's parents: [....] And lower to them the wing of humility out of mercy and say, "My Lord, have mercy upon them as they brought me up [when I was] small."

"Be neither miserly nor wasteful in one's expenditure: And give the relative his right, and [also] the poor and the traveller, and do not spend wastefully. (Quran 17:26)"

"Care for orphaned children: And do not approach the property of an orphan, except in the way that is best, until he reaches maturity...(Quran 17:34)

Keep one's promises: ...fulfil (every) engagement [i.e. promise/covenant], for (every) engagement will be questioned (on the Day of Reckoning). (Quran 17:34)

Be honest and fair in one's interactions: And give full measure when you measure, and weigh with an even balance. That is the best [way] and best in result. (Quran 17:35)

Do not be arrogant in one's claims or beliefs: And do not pursue that of which you have no knowledge. Indeed, the hearing, the sight and the heart - all those will be questioned. (Quran 17:36)

And do not walk upon the earth exultantly. Indeed, you will never tear the earth [apart], and you will never reach the mountains in height. (Quran 17:37)"

These few examples of practical, down-to-earth and, in themselves, humble instructions are absent from any set of instructions common in our society. Their simplicity but deep meaningfulness is a small sign of the elemental concept of Islamic life. They imply to "keep life simple". They concern everyday common events from which any height of achievement can follow, but without which all becomes built on sand.

An open opportunity

Islam is indeed both a religion and a movement, a blueprint for a way of life and living that sits well with the human psyche if a person allows himself to study its proposals objectively and at a human level. (Sheikh Abbas Jaffer – Islamic Sciences lecturer and teacher - 2019)

Ethics. From Mohammad to Mazzini. There is a common thread between these apparently distant and apparently contrasting human beings, which is that they both, like all thinkers who have turned their mind to the benefit of others, base their ideas on a principle of justice to be applied to the relationship between individuals in a community; justice which inevitably can only be reached if it works from ethic universal criteria born from the very human need for self-preservation, and not from any human principles of God or from human rules of market forces.

Although the idea of a return to the maligned canons of socialism, currently stuck in the doldrums of politics, is far from most people's minds (but never entirely gone away) one cannot resist correlating socialistic principles of equality, communality and the rejection of the capitalistic consumerist ideal with some of the basic principles of a book such as the Qur'an, the source of Islamic thought. But socialism is based on a system of laws imposing strict government controls, entirely absent in the Qur'an. It can be just a different kind of imposition, open to corruption and failure unless underpinned by a moral conviction. I find the example of the Qur'an interesting one because, once shorn of its obvious manifestations of representing a medieval culture, it is the source of rules of community living which is close to us, in spite having been isolated from the West for as long as its existence.

There can be no doubt that the strength of Islam is given by religious Faith. And having included all activities, actions and thought within their religious beliefs[vi] Islamic religion has become deeply inherent to its culture. We on the other hand can take inspiration from this by showing with full conviction, given to us by scientific research, and psychological understanding that these principles are in general correct, and necessary.

To anyone of a Christian perspective who has acquired even a superficial knowledge and confidence with what the Qur'an states, there are no real differences between the two outlooks. The differences are on one side the layers of interpretation of the Qur'an on the part of Muslim scholars over the centuries, and on the other, the layers of interpretation of Western thinkers and theologians over the principles laid out by Christ. Muhammad said he was not starting a new religion but "completing" the Bible. He termed Judaism, Christianity and Islam as the religions of "The Book", the Bible itself. His main issue with Christianity was the Divinity of Jesus which, from a purely historical perspective, and given the premises above, would appear to be a not unreasonable assumption.

In spite of all its faults which, both in terms of the past as well as the present, are certainly no worse than those of our own ostentatious West, and observed from a rational perspective of how its culture might be of use to our own, Islam inspires a coherent and well-used set of principles which might influence one's behaviour in life and begin to transform the Western rat-race and its fundamentally amoral attitude into a more caring, humane, and non-aggressive lifestyle. The cultural basis which makes this possible is the principle, affirmed in the Qur'an, of the need for the members of the community to be united, beyond any limitation imposed by tribe, country or religion. It is the concept of the Umma, which makes all Muslims brothers and sisters in principle and thus allows them to operate as a single group instead of as individuals. What the Qur'an preaches is not the conquest by force of the entire planet, but the importance of the recognition and the acceptance of universal teachings by all humanity. It is time that this wealth of thinking, currently shared by almost two billion people on the planet be made aware to the West. With a dose of overdue humility on our part, I believe we could learn a number of useful lessons on which to form a better and more promising, long-lasting society.

It would be foolish of me to be proposing a Utopia. From Plato onwards, no one (luckily) has been able to set one up. I am suggesting that we recognise the need to change to go forward, so our children can live a more significant and safer life. Change is possible. We have done it for millennia. Sometimes we have made important changes at the last minute, when all seemed lost or collapsing. We may need to do the same this time, because time is running out, on various fronts. This is just an encouragement not to be afraid of innovation. I am personally convinced that our extraordinarily creative, innovative Western mindset could bond and usefully fuse some aspects of at least the two cultures, achieving the beginning of another couple of thousand years of splendid civilisation.

Appendix, Further Reading, Notes & Bibliography

These notes are simply a few examples without any pretence of finality to illustrate how thinkers of different kinds, philosophers, and scientists, have addressed the concept of the existence of an element which can be defined as a God, a Power, or a Law. They also want to illustrate and give a feeling to the deeply human, wise and also forgiving nature of Islamic philosophy.

*

Pitfalls of modern society

Lord Dahrendorf, a member of the British Academy, outlines in a lecture on the pitfalls of modern society, some of the dilemmas and possible directions of society in the future[vii][2].

'Internationalised modern economies pose a social and political dilemma. In free societies, the search for competitiveness seems to damage social cohesion. If, on the other hand, such free societies choose to give social cohesion a higher priority, their competitiveness and with it their prosperity are at risk. Some countries, or at least their leaders, insist on competitiveness but do not want to sacrifice social cohesion and seem to achieve this by restricting political freedom. More and more people think that you can have two but not all three: prosperity and cohesion without freedom, prosperity and freedom without

---

[2] Lord Dahrendorf, Thank-offering to Britain Fund Lecture - Prosperity, Civility and Liberty: Can We Square the Circle? - The British Academy, 1996

civility, civility and freedom without prosperity. What would need to be done to square the circle?'

'The key to squaring the circle is strengthening, and in part rebuilding civil society. By civil society I mean that texture of our lives with others which does not need governments to sustain it because it is created by grass roots initiatives.'

'No word describes better the 'parts, interests and classes of citizens' which civil society is about than the word 'association'. The creative chaos of associations coalesces as if guided by an invisible hand into the settings in which the greatest number find the greatest life chances. In economic terms, the market describes that setting; in political terms, it is the public. Nowadays, both are mediated in numerous ways; the days of simple markets, or indeed of the public assembling outside the town hall for debate and decision, are almost gone. But the principles of both are still valid. The market and the public are where the associations of civil society interact.'

'In other words, there is such a thing as society.[3] What is more, there has to be if we do not want to end up in a state of anomie. The word, association, also indicates the necessary element of cohesion in civil society. Apart from the indispensable framework of the rule of law, the associations of civil society represent values of trust and cooperation, and of inclusion. A civil society is a society of citizens who have rights and accept obligations, and who behave in a civil and civilised manner toward each other. It is a society which tries to make sure that no one is excluded, and which offers its members a sense of belonging as well as a constitution of liberty.'

---

[3] This is a reference to Margaret Thatcher's phrase 'there is no such thing as society'.

Lord Dahrendorf's conclusions, and his prescription for strengthening and rebuilding society are less than convincing, are unconvincing, since they are limited to suggesting that companies should be of 'a variety of sizes', and a combination of 'competitiveness and stakeholder involvement'.

'This is actually what many companies are groping for today, and the best provide benchmarks for the rest. Individuals have to respond to the analogous dual challenge of flexibility and security. People's lives will look different that they did in the days of old-style careers in an expectation of full employment. Security is no longer built into the world of work, or of education for that matter. People have to carry it with and within them which means their entitlements have to be transportable, and their strength lies in their skills that include the ability to go on adjusting and enhancing them. There are signs that women find it easier to cope with the new balance of flexibility and security than men; perhaps they had to do so earlier. In institutional as well as personal terms, associations in the narrow and the organised sense will play a major part. The tradition of voluntarism, of volunteering as well as charitable giving will see a new flowering. The result will be untidy and imperfect, it will not do away with pain and fear, or with conflict, but it may point the way to a prosperous, civil and liberal world.'

(Dahrendorf, Ralf (1929-2009). German sociologist)

I have quoted Lord Dahrendorf at length because he gives a succinct description of the dilemmas faced by society world-wide. Since the demise of the Soviet Union and Communism, and the consequent need to choose between two alignments available, individual societies have been at liberty to follow their own inclinations in the way they develop, producing solutions which are sometimes middle of the road between capitalism and authoritarianism.

Lord Dahrendorf also appears to pin-point the problem accurately, but then fails to draw the obvious conclusions: for if the way to square the circle is to enhance social cohesion through association, what better form of association than the local community?

*

Speech of Giuseppe Mazzini in New York 1858

The value of this speech lies in the fact that is has been uttered by a politician, not a philosopher, or a preacher, in the middle of the 19th century.

"I intend to speak to you of your duties. I intend to speak to you, according to the dictates of my heart, of the holiest things we know; to speak to you of God, of Humanity, of the Fatherland, and the Family.

Listen to me in love, as I shall speak to you in love. My words are words of conviction, matured by long years of study, of experience, and of sorrow. The duties which I point out to you I have striven, and shall strive while I live, to fulfil so far as I have the power. I may err, but my error is not of the heart. I may deceive myself, but I will not deceive you. Listen to me, then, fraternally; judge freely among yourselves whether I speak truth or error. If it seems to you I speak error, leave me; but follow me and act according to my teachings, if you believe me the apostle of truth. To err is misfortune and deserving of commiseration; but to know the truth and fail to regulate our actions according to its teachings [Page 6] is a crime condemned alike by Heaven and earth.

Wherefore do I speak to you of your duties before speaking to you of your rights? Wherefore, in a Society wherein all, voluntarily or involuntarily, tend to oppress you; wherein the exercise of so many of the rights that belong to man is continually denied to you; wherein your portion is suffering, and all that which men call happiness is for other classes - do I speak to you of self-sacrifice rather than of conquest? of virtue, of moral improvement, and of education, rather than of material well-being?

All that has been achieved or attempted in the cause of progress and improvement in Europe during the last fifty years, whether against absolute governments or the aristocracy of birth, has been attempted in the name of the Rights of Man and of Liberty, as the means of that well-being which has been regarded as the end and aim of life. All the acts of the great French Revolution, and of all of those revolutions which succeeded and imitated it, were a consequence of the "Declaration of the Rights of Man." All the works of those philosophers, whose writings prepared the way for that Revolution, were founded upon a theory of Liberty, and of making known to every individual his Rights. The doctrines of all the Revolutionary schools preached that man was born for happiness; that he had a right to seek happiness by every means in his power; and that no one had a right to impede him in that search; while he had a right to overthrow whatever obstacles he met in his path towards it. And all those obstacles were overthrown; liberty was achieved.
[.....] Has the condition of the people improved? Have the millions who live by the daily labour of their hands acquired any, the smallest amount, of the promised and desired well-being?
No; the condition of the people is not improved. (.....) In almost all countries the condition of the workingman has become more uncertain, more precarious, while those crises which condemn thousands of workingmen to a certain period of inertia have become more frequent.

And nevertheless in these last fifty years the sources of social wealth and the mass of material means of happiness have been continually on the increase. Commerce, surmounting those frequent crises which are inevitable in the absolute absence of all organization, has achieved an increase of power and activity, and a wider sphere of operation. Communication has almost everywhere been rendered rapid and secure, and hence the price of produce has decreased in proportion to the diminished cost of transport.

On the other hand, the idea that there are rights inherent to human nature is now generally admitted and accepted - hypocritically and in words at least - even by those who seek to withhold those rights. Why, then, has not the condition of the people improved? Why has the consumption of produce, instead of being equally distributed among all the Members of European Society, become concentrated in the hands of a few, of a class forming a new aristocracy? Why has the fresh impulse given to industry and commerce resulted, not in the well-being of the many, but in the luxury of a few?

The answer is clear to those who look closely into things. Men are the creatures of education, and their actions are but the consequence of the principle of education given to them. The promoters of revolutions and political transformations have hitherto founded them all on one idea, the idea of the rights pertaining to the individual. Those revolutions achieved Liberty - individual liberty, liberty of education, liberty of belief, liberty of commerce, liberty in all things and for all men.

But of what use were rights when acquired by men who had not the means of exercising them? Of what use was mere liberty of education to men who had neither time nor means to profit by it? Of what use was mere liberty of commerce to those who possessed neither merchandise, capital, nor credit?

In all the countries wherein these principles were proclaimed, Society was composed of the small number of individuals who were possessors of the land, of capital, and of credit, and of the vast multitude who possessed nothing

but the labour of their hands, and were compelled to sell that labour to the first class on any terms, in order to live. For such men, compelled to spend the whole day in material and monotonous exertion, and condemned to a continual struggle against
hunger and want, what was liberty but an illusion, a bitter irony?
The only way to prevent this state of things would have been for the upper classes voluntarily to consent to reduce the hours of labour, while they increased its remuneration; to bestow an uniform and gratuitous education upon the multitude; to render the instruments of labour accessible to all, and create a credit for workmen of good capacity and of good intentions.
Now, why should they have done this? Was not well-being the end and aim of life? Was not prosperity the one thing desired by all? Why should they diminish their own enjoyments in favour of others? "Let those help themselves who can. When Society has secured to each individual the free exercise of those rights which are inherent in human nature, it has done all it is bound to do. If there be any one who, from some fatality of his own position, is unable to exercise any of these rights, let him resign himself to his fate, and not blame others."
It was natural they should speak thus, and thus in fact they spoke. And this mode of regarding the poor by the privileged classes soon became the mode in which individuals regarded one another. Each man occupied himself with his own rights and the amelioration of his own position, without seeking to provide for others; and when those rights clashed with the rights of others, the result was a state of war - a war, not of blood, but of gold and craft; less manly than the other, but equally fatal; a relentless war in which those who possessed means inexorably crushed the weak and inexpert.
In this state of continual warfare, men were educated in selfishness and the exclusive greed of material well-being. Mere liberty of belief had destroyed all community of faith; mere liberty of education generated moral anarchy.

*Mankind, without any common bond, without unity of religious belief or aim, bent upon enjoyment and
naught beyond, sought each and all to tread in their own path, little heeding if, in pursuing it, they trampled upon the bodies of their brothers - brothers in name, but enemies in fact. This is the state of things we have reached at the present day, thanks to the theory of rights.*

Rights no doubt exist; but when the rights of one individual happen to clash with those of another, how can we hope to reconcile and harmonize them, if we do not refer to something which is above all rights? And when the rights of an individual, or of many individuals, clash with the rights of the country, to what tribunal shall we appeal?
If the right to the greatest possible amount of happiness exist in all human beings, how are we to solve the question between the workingman and the manufacturer? If the right to existence is the first inviolable right of every man, who shall demand the sacrifice of that existence for the benefit of other men?
Will you demand it in the name of the country, of Society, of the multitude, your brothers?
What is their country to those who hold the theory I describe, if it be not the spot wherein their individual rights are most secure? What is Society but an assemblage of men who have agreed to bring the power of the many in support of the rights of each?
And you, who for fifty years have been preaching to the individual that Society is constituted for the purpose of securing to him the exercise of his rights, how can you ask him to sacrifice them all in favour of that Society, and submit, if need be, to ceaseless effort, to imprisonment or exile, for the sake of improving it? After having taught him by every means in your power that the end and aim of life is happiness, how can you expect him to sacrifice both happiness and life itself to free his country from foreign oppression, or to produce some amelioration in the condition of a class to which he does not belong? After you have

preached to him for years in the name of material interest, can you pretend that he shall see wealth and power within his own reach and not stretch forth his hand to grasp them, even though to the injury of his fellow-men?

Who shall persuade the man, believing solely in the theory of rights, that he is bound to strive for the common good, and occupy himself in the development of the social idea? Suppose he should rebel; suppose he should feel himself strong enough to say to you: "I break the social bond; my tendencies and my faculties invite me

elsewhere; *I have a sacred, an inviolable right to develop those tendencies and faculties, and I choose to be at war with the rest;" what answer can you make him within the limits of the Doctrine of Rights? What right have you, merely as a majority, to compel his obedience to laws which do not accord with his individual desires and aspirations? What right have you to punish him should he violate those laws?*

The Rights of each individual are equal; the mere fact of living together in Society does not create a single one. Society has greater power, not greater rights, than the individual. How, then, will you prove to the individual that he is bound to confound his will in the will of his brothers, whether of country or of humanity? By means of the prison or the executioner? Every Society that has existed hitherto has employed these means.

But this is a state of war, and we need peace; this is tyrannical repression, and we need Education.

Education, I have said, and my whole doctrine is included and summed up in this grand word. The vital question in agitation at the present day is a question of Education. We do not seek to establish a new order of things through violence. Any order of things established through violence, even though itself superior to the old, is still a tyranny. What we have to do is to propose, for the approval of the nation, an order of things which we believe to be superior to that now existing, and to educate men by every possible means to develop it and act in accordance with it.

The theory of Rights may suffice to arouse men to overthrow the obstacles placed in their path by tyranny, but it is impotent where the object in view is to create a noble and powerful harmony between the various elements of which the nation is composed. With the theory of happiness as the primary aim of existence, we shall only produce egoists who will carry the old passions and desires into the new order of things, and introduce corruption into it a few months after. We have, therefore, to seek a Principle of Education superior to any such theory, and capable of guiding mankind onwards toward their own improvement, of teaching them constancy and self-sacrifice, and of uniting them with their fellow-men, without making them dependent either on the idea of a single man or the force of the majority.

This principle is DUTY. We must convince men that they are all sons of one sole God, and bound to fulfil and execute one sole law here on earth; that each of them is bound to live, not for himself, but for others; that the aim of existence is not to be more or less happy, but to make ourselves and others more virtuous; that to struggle against injustice and error (wherever they exist), in the name and for the benefit of their brothers, is not only a right but a Duty; a duty which may not be neglected without sin; the duty of their whole life.

(......)

Improve yourselves! Let this be the aim of your life. It is only by improving yourselves, by becoming more virtuous, that you can render your position lastingly less unhappy. Petty tyrants would arise among yourselves by thousands, so long as you should merely strive to advance in the name of material interests or a special social organization. A change of social organization is of little moment while you yourselves remain with your present passions and selfishness. Social organizations are like certain plants which yield either poison or medicine according to the mode in which they are administered. Good men can work good even out of an evil organization, and evil men can work evil out of good organizations.

"*(.......)*

But, be warned! and believe the words of a man who has been earnestly studying the course of events in Europe during the last thirty years, and who has seen the holiest enterprises fail in the hour of promised success through the errors or immorality of their supporters. You will never succeed unless through [Page 141] your own improvement. You can only obtain the exercise of your rights by deserving them through your own activity and your own spirit of love and sacrifice. If you seek your rights in the name of duties fulfilled or to fulfil, you will obtain them. If you seek them in the name of selfishness, or any theory of happiness and well-being propounded by the teachers of materialism, you will never achieve other than a momentary triumph, to be followed by utter delusion.

They who appeal to you in the name of well-being and happiness, will deceive and betray you. They seek only their own well-being and happiness, and merely desire to unite with you as an element of strength wherewith to overcome the obstacles in their own path. When once they have obtained their own rights through your help, they will abandon the effort to obtain yours in order to enjoy their own. Such is the history of the last half-century, and the name of this last half-century is, materialism.

Sad story of blood and sorrow! I have seen them in my own land - these men who denied God, religion, virtue, and sacrifice, and spoke only in the name of the right to happiness and enjoyment--I have seen them advance boldly to the struggle with the words People and Liberty on their lips, and unite with us men of a better faith, who imprudently admitted them in our ranks. As soon as a first victory, or the opportunity of some cowardly compromise, opened the path of enjoyment to them, they forsook the cause of the people, and became our bitterest enemies the day after. A few years of danger and persecution were sufficient to weary and discourage them.

And wherefore should they, men without any conscientious belief in a Law of Duty, without faith in a mission imposed upon man by a Supreme Power, have persisted in sacrifice even to the last years of life?

And I have seen, with deep sadness, the sons of the people, educated in materialism by those men, turn false to their mission and their future, false to their country and themselves, betrayed by some foolish, immoral hope of obtaining material happiness, through furthering the caprice or interest of a despotism.

I have seen the workingmen of France stand by, indifferent spectators of the coup d'état of the second of December, because all the great social questions had dwindled in their minds into a question of material prosperity; and they foolishly believed that the promises, artfully made to them by him who had destroyed the liberty of their country, would be kept. Now they mourn over their lost liberty, without having acquired even the promised material well-being.

No; without God, without the sense of a moral law, without morality, without a spirit of sacrifice, and by merely following after men who have neither faith, nor reverence for truth, nor holiness of life, nor ought to guide them but the vanity of their own systems - I repeat it with deep conviction - you will never succeed. You may achieve émeutes, but you will never realize the true Great Revolution you and I alike desire - a revolution, not the offspring and illusion of irritated selfishness, but of religious conviction. Your own improvement and that of others; this must be the supreme hope and aim of every social transformation.

You cannot change the fate of man by merely embellishing his material dwelling. You will never induce the society to which you belong to substitute a system of Association for a system of salary and wages, unless you convince them that your association will result in improved production and collective prosperity. And you can only prove this by showing yourselves capable of founding and maintaining associations through your own honesty, mutual good-will, love of labour, and capacity of self-sacrifice.

In order to progress, you must show yourselves capable of progress. Tradition, Progress, Association. These three things are sacred.
[....]

(Giuseppe Mazzini, An Essay On the Duties of Man Addressed to Workingmen in New York in 1858.
Published by Funk & Wagnalls, 1898)

*

What is the Ideal Unemployment Rate?

Unemployment is considered to be one of the biggest social evils that is affecting our lives today. Its economic impact is not as important as its social impact. Most people in society today depend upon jobs to earn their living. Therefore, any scenario which negatively affects the jobs of these millions of people will affect the fabric of the entire society as a whole.

Hence, we are sure about one thing i.e. unemployment is a bad thing and that it must be eradicated. However, what constitutes the word eradicated is not clearly understood. Should unemployment be managed at a given level or should it be completely removed from society? The answers to these questions are complex and therefore we will deal with them in the rest of this article.

The Prevalent Viewpoint

The prevalent viewpoint in the world is that unemployment cannot and should not be completely eradicated. This notion stems from the fact that zero unemployment is an impractical goal. This goal has been followed for many decades by communist countries and the result was utter chaos and economic mayhem. The more conservative point of view suggests that unemployment is like a necessary by-product of the modern economic system. However, it must be managed within its current levels. Failure to manage this unemployment creates problems. However, eradicating it completely is not an option at all.

This brings us to another question as to what is that optimum level of unemployment that a government must try to obtain. The answer to this isn't straightforward either. There is no hard and fast rule that can be applied to all economies at all points of time. There are a multitude of variables that play a part in the unemployment rate. Hence, the only logical conclusion is to compare the performance of an economy to that of its peers. Most developed countries will be facing similar economic conditions and hence their unemployment rates can be compared with one another and the same logic can be applied to developing as well as third world countries.

Hence, according to modern theory, the ideal unemployment rate is not a static goal. Rather it is a dynamic goal that changes in accordance with the current situation.

Why Manage Unemployment?

Economic theory has seen many hardliners who were obsessed with the idea of zero unemployment. Their logic was that economies exist to provide human needs and serve humans. The biggest way in which they serve humans is by providing employment. Hence, zero unemployment must be the foremost (if not the only) objective driving economic policy creation. Such ideas found patronage in communist societies worldwide. However, if one sees beyond the basic argument, the flaws are readily apparent. The most obvious ones have been listed below:

- *Types of Unemployment: The modern economic system does not define unemployment as a single term. This means that not all types of unemployment belong to one and the same category. Rather economists have created multiple categories to segregate unemployment caused by different root causes. We will learn about them in the next few articles. However, for the moment, it needs to be understood that some forms of unemployment are indeed voluntary or beneficial. This is the unemployment caused when people need to re-skill themselves to meet the needs of a changing economic environment. Also, some people may want to spend more time being unemployed till they find a job that matches their skill sets.*

The government cannot eradicate these types of unemployment until and unless it encroaches on the rights of the employers and the employees to make their own decisions. Since we live in a free market, this is not possible. Hence, the word "unemployment" as it is currently defined will always be a part and parcel of life.

- *100% Percent Employment and Growth. Secondly our economic system is built on the notion of perpetual economic growth. Human resources are one of the biggest factors contributing to growth. If the human resources are 100% employed, where does it leave room for growth? How can an economy grow when one of the inputs required for growth has been exhausted?*

Conclusion

Hence, it would be safe to say that the modern approach of comparing the unemployment rates with peers is relatively better than pursuing the utopian goal of 100% employment. There are some drawbacks to the peer evaluation approach as well. However, they can be managed relatively painlessly and this method is definitely the better of the two evils.

Prachi Juneja - Reviewed By Management Study Guide Content - www.managementstudyguide.com/- 2015

*

Antonio Gramsci

The Italian philosopher Antonio Gramsci proposed from his prison cell that we conceive of "religion taken not in the confessional sense but in the secular sense of a unity of faith between a conception of the world and a corresponding norm of conduct," and then went on to ask, "Why call this unity of faith 'religion' and not 'ideology,' or even 'politics'?" (p. 183. Antonio Gramsci, "The Study of Philosophy," in Selections from the Prison Notebooks)

*

Immanuel Kant

Immanuel Kant (1724–1804) is a central figure in modern philosophy. He synthesized early modern rationalism and empiricism, set the terms for much of nineteenth and twentieth century philosophy, and continues to exercise a significant influence today in metaphysics, epistemology, ethics, political philosophy, aesthetics, and other fields. The fundamental idea of Kant's "critical philosophy" — especially in his three Critiques: the Critique of Pure Reason (1781, 1787), the Critique of Practical Reason (1788), and the Critique of the Power of Judgment (1790) — is human autonomy. He argues that the *"the source of human understanding are the general laws of nature that structure all our experience; and that human reason gives itself the moral law, which is our basis for belief in God, freedom, and immortality. Therefore, scientific knowledge,*

morality, and religious belief are mutually consistent and secure because they all rest on the same foundation of human autonomy, which is also the final end of nature according to the teleological worldview of reflecting judgment that Kant introduces to unify the theoretical and practical parts of his philosophical system."
E. Kant – Critique of Pure Reason)

*

Teilhard de Chardin

Catholic dissident theologian, the Jesuit priest Teilhardn de Chardin has an intriguing and instinctively convincing view in this respect: *"The spiritualists are right when they defend a certain transcendence of Man over Nature. The materialists are not wrong either when they affirm that Man is nothing but another being among the series of animal forms. For the two antithetical affirmations are resolved in a [hypothetical] 'movement'. For from the cell to the thinking animal, as from the atom to the cell, a similar process of "raising of the temperature of psychic concentration" occurs [...which induces intelligence].*

Also: *"Teilhard's concept is that the continuity of Evolution is expressed in a progression of 'psychic concentration'. The consummation of the individual induced by the principle of convergence which informs Evolution is achieved through the consummated Being, which is Spirit, known as God. A Centre of universal consciousness shines over the summit of Evolution. Teilhard forcibly states that "... in the truest sense of the term, Cosmic (Conscience) is a form of love, and cannot be other." And he adds: " In the Cosmos as I have described it here, unlikely as this expression may seem, it becomes possible to love the Universe. And it is only in this act itself that love can develop a clarity and a power without limits."*

(Petite vie de Pierre Teilhard de Chardin - By Bernard Sesé, Maurice Ernst)

*

Stephen Hawkin

In his "A Short History of Time" is also drawn to a sense of Universal power: *"[...] if we do discover a complete theory, it should in time be understandable in broad principle by everyone, not just a few scientists. Then we shall all, philosophers, scientists, and just ordinary people, be able to take part in the discussion of the question of why it is that we and the universe exist. If we find the answer to that, it would be the ultimate triumph of human reason – for then we would know the mind of God."*
(Stephen Hawkin, A Brief History of Time)

*

Akeel Bilgrami

The Columbia University philosopher, Akeel Bilgrami, despite being an atheist, does not completely reject the scope of religion having a critically instructive role in our time. As he says, *"religion is not primarily a matter of belief and doctrine but about the sense of community and shared values that it can sometimes provide in contexts where other forms of solidarity—such as a strong labor movement—are missing, and it sometimes provides a moral perspective for a humane politic as it did in the liberation theology movement in Central America."*

*

Spinoza - "Nothing exists but God",

[…] consequently, Nature does not work with an end in view. For the eternal and infinite Being, which we call God or Nature, acts by the same necessity as that whereby it exists […]. Therefore, as He does not exist for the sake of an end, so neither does He act for the sake of an end; of His existence and of His action there is neither origin nor end. [iv. Preface]. God is indifferent to individuals. God is without passions, neither is he affected by any emotion of pleasure or pain. Strictly speaking, God does not love anyone. [V.17]. He who loves God cannot endeavor that God should love him in return. ([V.19]. **(Spinoza)**

*

New Horizons

Many challenges in today's world, make us think about what it means to be Muslim and what it means to be citizen of our country. One thing that has struck me is the unveiling of how women have been treated in our society. Muslim and not Muslim. The government, the charity sector scandals. Our constant message is that we need to step back and not be challenged by these things, thanks to our religion. If we are consumed, we become a part of the problem and we don't hold the moral agency.
We need to think about Islam in a different way. As it has always been. At the beginning it was that (the Prophet) was an agent with a critical voice saying Islam means to make

whole, to bring something back to its wholeness. So we don't need to change Islam, but to take a different approach.

The Quran tells us that we must change ourselves. Unless I start with myself [....] then I can have no hope of changing all the big things around me.

Islam for us is a continuous flowing of a fresh spring. But to retain its freshness it needs to keep speaking to us and we need to keep listening to it; so not the voice of Islam 200 or 1000 years ago or even 50 or ten years ago; we must continually go back to this well [...] so we can continue to have a fresh take on that valid religion. Keep reading, keep interpreting our religion. Because religion is only a human interpretation, so we need to go back to our interpretation, and ask questions as the environment changes.

The third point I make is when you look at our program, the people sitting here, we realize that the challenge for us is so great thinking about Islam in our own bubble, thinking just for ourselves within ourselves is no longer a tenable way forward. We need to open up our doors and ensure that this conversation on Islam is something that everybody has a stake in, believers non-believers, the table has to be open to bring their ideas to the table. In order to learn where things have gone wrong. I think that's why when the Quran addresses its readers it addresses humanity.
This is our cup of tea and we have a right to our cup of tea.

(Dilwar Hussain – opening speech at British Islam Conference, London 2018)

*

Islam goes beyond nationalities.

Nation-states and the principle of nationhood have been created around 500 years ago. Are they becoming once more obsolete? With globalisation the rulers of the game are already the corporations, virtually above the law and setting their conditions to many so called 'independent' countries.

*

Orientalist' view of Islam

We must address the 'Orientalist' view of Islam as being a manifestation of a culture which is traditionally characterised as slothful, despotic, sensual, backward, and so on. We must address it not to demonstrate the contrary but rather to intelligently weave the differences between cultures into a positive manifestation of how life can be lived.

*

From "What Is Islam" – Contradiction in Islam –

In addressing the question of how to conceptualize Islam as a unity in light of diversity, the purpose [.........] has been threefold. First, to demonstrate to the reader that in relation to Islam, we are actually talking not so much about conceptualizing unity in the face of diversity, but rather about conceptualizing unity in the face of
outright contradiction. Second, it has been to re- orient the historical consciousness of the reader
to awareness of the fact that these contradictory claims by Muslims about the
normative constitution of Islam were claims made, not on the [....] margins of the Muslims' discourses about Islam, [....]

but rather at the very social and political and intellectual centre of Muslims' discourses about Islam. [......] Third, it has been to plant the seed in the mind of the reader that these contradictions cannot meaningfully be understood, as they generally are, by separating them out as differences between the religious and cultural (or religious and secular) spheres of something called Islam [....]. Rather, I suggest
that these contradictions call for—indeed, demand and require—a suspension of these received categories of distinction in order to reconceptualize Islam as
a human and historical phenomenon in new terms.

Shahab Ahmed – What is Islam? – The Importance of Being Islamic

*

Al-Andalus

The eight centuries from late 600AD to 1500AD when most of the Mediterranean coastline was successfully run by the Arabs must not be used as an excuse for nostalgia by contemporary Muslims but serve as an example of how Islam can be seen to have the capabilities for a positive and fruitful culture which sowed the seeds for the European Renaissance and was destroyed by the extreme and uncompromising forces of the Inquisition. etc.

*

Bibliography

Undoing the Demos: Neoliberalism's Stealth Revolution - By Wendy Brown – Zone Books - 2017

The Message of the Qur'an – Muhammad Asad – The Book Foundation – 2012

The Tyranny of Merit - by Michael J. Sandel -2020 - ISBN 9780241407592

Age of Extremes, by Eric Hobsbaum

What is Islam?: The Importance of Being Islamic – by Shahab Ahmed - Princeton University Press – 2017

Wasted Lives – Modernity and its Outcasts – by Zygmunt Bauman – Polity Press, Cambridge - 2004

Antonio Gramsci, "The Study of Philosophy," in, Selections from the Prison Notebooks

Goethe The Muslim. dr. Katharina Mommsen - Reference: Read in PDF file: 1967-The Muslim

I Diritti di Dio – Le cinque sfide dell'Islam all'Occidente – Ciro Sbailo' = libreriauniversitaria.it – 2016

George Monbiot, *How Did We Get Into This Mess?* Verso, 2016

Sotto il suo passo nascono i fiori. Goethe e l'Islam - Pietrangelo Buttafuoco, Francesca Bocca-Aldaqre

https://en.wikipedia.org/wiki/Islamic_ethics

https://www.tandfonline.com/doi/abs/10.1080/0305724970260403?journalCode=cjme20

Karen Armstrong – Muhammad, Prophet of Our Time – Harper Press – 2006

The Crisis of the Meritocracy - Peter Mandler. Oxford University Press, November 2020. pp. 384

Flailing States - Pankaj Mishra on Anglo-America – LRB, July 2020

Lewis, Bernard (1994), *Race and Slavery in the Middle East,* Oxford University Press

John Gray, *Feline Philosophy, Cats and the Meaning of Life.*

Homo Deus, by Yuval oah Harari.

Elite schools breed entitlement, entrench inequality—and then pretend to be engines of social change. Story by <u>Caitlin Flanagan</u> The Atlantic – April 2021 issue

Notes

[i] *Giuseppe Mazzini - An essay on the duties of man.*

[ii] *Spirituality; "[....] Modern usages tend to refer to a subjective experience of a sacred dimension and the "deepest values and meanings by which people live", often in a context separate from organized religious institutions. [...] After the Second World War, spirituality and theistic religion became increasingly disconnected, and spirituality became more oriented on subjective experience, instead of "attempts to place the self within a broader ontological context." (Gerard Saucier - Professor of Psychology, University of Oregon – 2006)*

[iii] *See Bibliography*

[iv] *I could not think of a better name. In spite of its totally misleading meaning of Information Technology. Suggestions welcome.*

[v] *Once again – I apologize for the use of the IT; its automatic and unavoidable connotation probably make it sound ridiculous. Truth is |I have not been able to find of a better solution.*

[vi] *But to understand the true meaning of this and its exemptions, variations please see 'What Is Islam'*

[vii] *A fascinating subject in itself, to establish how the human race has come to establish that the preservation of its species was better protected by humanity (humanness) and collaboration rather than from a principle of sheer aggressiveness*

London, March 2021.

Printed in Great Britain
by Amazon